EXTREME WEATHER

Droughts

by Anne Wendorff

Consultant:
Mark Seeley, Ph.D.
University of Minnesota Extension
Meteorologist and Climatologist,
Department of Soil, Water, and Climate,
St Paul, Minn.

BLASTOFF!
4
READERS

BELLWETHER MEDIA • MINNEAPOLIS, MN

Note to Librarians, Teachers, and Parents:

Blastoff! Readers are carefully developed by literacy experts and combine standards-based content with developmentally appropriate text.

Level 1 provides the most support through repetition of high-frequency words, light text, predictable sentence patterns, and strong visual support.

Level 2 offers early readers a bit more challenge through varied simple sentences, increased text load, and less repetition of high-frequency words.

Level 3 advances early-fluent readers toward fluency through increased text and concept load, less reliance on visuals, longer sentences, and more literary language.

Level 4 builds reading stamina by providing more text per page, increased use of punctuation, greater variation in sentence patterns, and increasingly challenging vocabulary.

Level 5 encourages children to move from "learning to read" to "reading to learn" by providing even more text, varied writing styles, and less familiar topics.

Whichever book is right for your reader, Blastoff! Readers are the perfect books to build confidence and encourage a love of reading that will last a lifetime!

This edition first published in 2009 by Bellwether Media.

No part of this publication may be reproduced in whole or in part without written permission of the publisher. For information regarding permission, write to Bellwether Media Inc., Attention: Permissions Department, Post Office Box 19349, Minneapolis, MN 55419.

Library of Congress Cataloging-in-Publication Data
Wendorff, Anne.
  Droughts / by Anne Wendorff.
    p. cm. — (Blastoff! readers: Extreme weather)
  Includes bibliographical references and index.
  Summary: "Simple text and full color photographs introduce beginning readers to the characteristics of droughts. Developed by literacy experts for students in kindergarten through third grade"—Provided by publisher.
  ISBN-13: 978-1-60014-184-3 (hardcover : alk. paper)
  ISBN-10: 1-60014-184-6 (hardcover : alk. paper)
  1. Droughts—Juvenile literature. I. Title.

  QC929.25.W46 2008
  551.57'73—dc22   2008015217

Contents

What Is a Drought?   4

The Effects of a Drought   12

Conserving Water   20

Glossary   22

To Learn More   23

Index   24

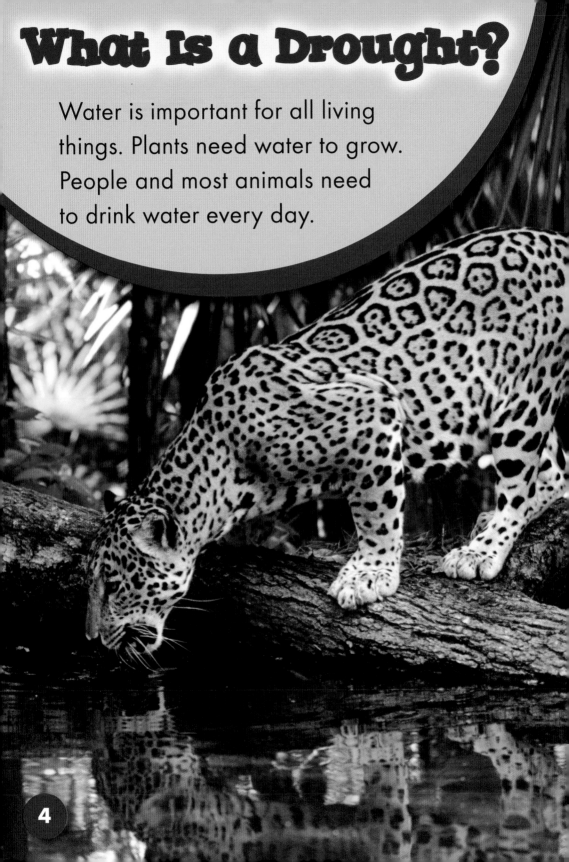

What Is a Drought?

Water is important for all living things. Plants need water to grow. People and most animals need to drink water every day.

In most places, there is enough water to meet the needs of living things. It falls from the sky as rain or snow. It fills rivers, lakes, and ponds.

Sometimes a place receives far less rainfall than usual. Then plants and animals do not have enough water. A time of unusually dry weather that lasts for many months or longer is called a drought. It can be a difficult and even dangerous time for living things.

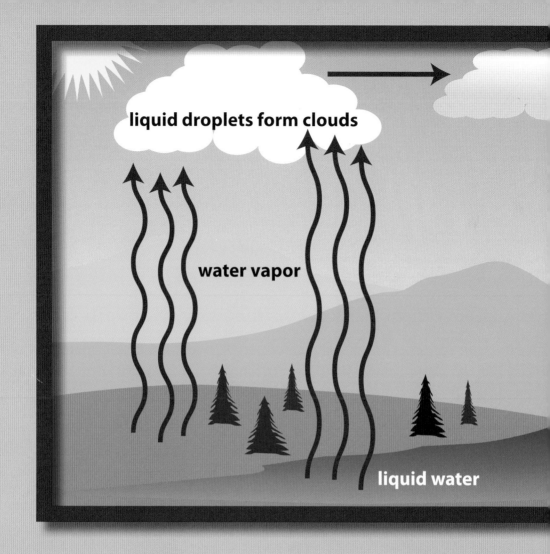

liquid droplets form clouds

water vapor

liquid water

Water normally moves constantly through a **water cycle**. **Liquid** water turns into a **gas** called **water vapor**. It rises in the sky, where the temperatures are cooler, and turns into liquid droplets. These droplets form clouds.

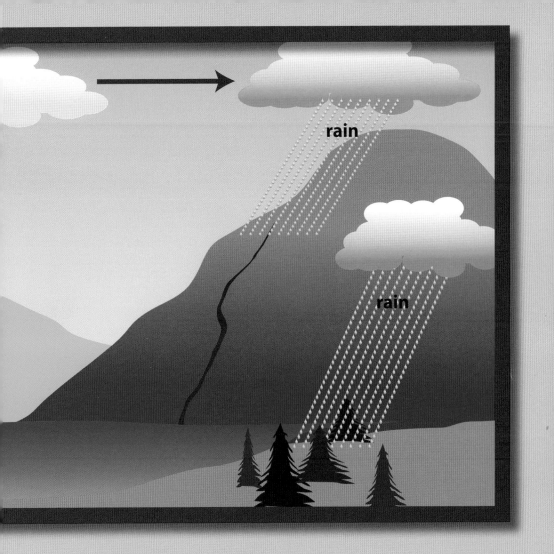

rain

rain

Eventually they fall back to Earth as rain. The rainwater will then turn into water vapor and rise again.

A drought happens when the water cycle is broken and it doesn't rain for weeks. It is often difficult to predict when a drought will happen or how long it will last.

Scientists know that droughts can happen when **air pressure** is high and prevents water vapor from rising into the sky to form clouds.

Air pressure is the force of air pressing down on everything. When water vapor cannot rise to form clouds, it cannot return to Earth as rain or snow.

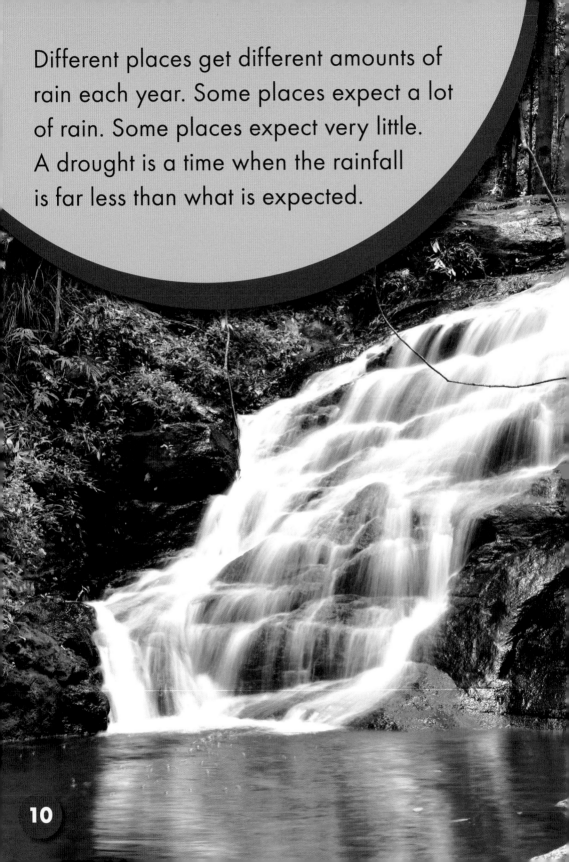

Different places get different amounts of rain each year. Some places expect a lot of rain. Some places expect very little. A drought is a time when the rainfall is far less than what is expected.

This can happen in places that are normally rainy or places that are normally dry.

The Effects of a Drought

Some droughts are mild and last only a short time. Other droughts are more serious.

A serious drought creates many problems. It makes the soil very dry. Plants need water in the soil to grow. They dry up and die quickly without moisture. Farmers can lose an entire **crop** in a drought. Dry soil is easily blown by the wind. Blowing soil can fill the air in a drought. This is called a **dust storm**.

Severe droughts can cause **famine**. This means there is not enough food for people to eat. People may die of hunger. This kind of drought is considered a **disaster**.

In severe droughts, the water in rivers, ponds, and lakes may dry up.

Animals may not be able to find enough to eat or drink in a drought. They can become sick and die.

A severe drought can affect a large area and last for years. This occurred in the American Midwest in the 1930s. A drought lasted more than seven years. Many families had to leave their homes to find water.

The area became known as "The Dust Bowl" because of the severe dust storms that occurred during this drought.

Conserving Water

People may have to take special steps to **conserve** water during a drought. People can avoid watering lawns or washing cars.

It is important not to waste water at any time, but especially during a drought. Water is a precious **resource**.

Glossary

air pressure—the force of the air pressing down

conserve—to use less water so the water supply lasts longer

crop—the amount of food produced in a single harvest

disaster—an event that causes great damage or suffering

dust storm—dry soil blown around by the wind; dust storms are common during droughts.

famine—a serious lack of food

gas—a form of matter with no definite shape; gas can fill up any space.

liquid—a form of matter with no definite shape; liquid can spill or flow.

resource—something valuable or useful to people

water cycle—the constant movement of Earth's water; water rises into the air, then falls back to Earth.

water vapor—the gaseous form of water; water vapor rises into the air as part of the water cycle.

To Learn More

AT THE LIBRARY

Cooper, Michael. *Dust to Eat: Drought and Depression in the 1930's*. New York: Clarion Books, 2004.

Olson, Nathan. *Droughts*. Mankato, Minn.: Coughlan, 2005.

Woods, Mary and Michael. *Droughts*. Minneapolis, Minn.: Lerner, 2006.

ON THE WEB
Learning more about droughts is as easy as 1, 2, 3.

1. Go to www.factsurfer.com

2. Enter "droughts" into search box.

3. Click the "Surf" button and you will see a list of related web sites.

With factsurfer.com, finding more information is just a click away.

Index

1930s, 18
air pressure, 8, 9
American Midwest, 18
animals, 4, 17
clouds, 6
conservation, 20, 21
crop, 13
disaster, 15
Dust Bowl, The, 19
dust storm, 13, 19
famine, 15
farmers, 13
gas, 6
invisible drought, 9
lakes, 5, 16, 17
liquid, 6, 17
plants, 4, 5, 9, 13
ponds, 5, 16, 17
rainfall, 5, 7, 10
resource, 21
rivers, 5, 16

scientists, 8
soil, 13
water cycle, 6, 7
water vapor, 6, 7, 9, 17

The images in this book are reproduced through the courtesy of: Andrey Ukhov, front cover; Gerry Ellis / Getty Images, pp. 4-5; Linda Clavel, pp. 6-7; coko, pp. 8-9; Juan Martinez, pp. 10-11; Jeff Hunter / Getty Images, p. 11 (inset); Aninka, p. 12; Getty Images, pp. 13, 14-15, 18; Clint Spencer, p. 15 (inset); Jonathan Heger, pp. 16-17; Time & Life Pictures / Getty Images, p. 19; AFP / Getty Images, p.20 (inset); Tony Dawson / Getty Images, pp. 20-21.